DETROIT PUBLIC LIBRARY

3 5674 00197221 6

RELEASED FROM
DETROIT PUBLIC LIBRARY

D1316828

DETROIT PUBLIC LIBRARY

PLEASE RETURN TO KNAPP BRANCH LIBRARY
13330 CONANT   DETROIT, MI 48212
876-0133

DATE DUE

FEB 19 1992

FEB 03 1994

MAY 09 1994

FEB 2 1 1995

APR 1 0 1997

MAR 2 5 1999

03

A BOOK OF DRAGONS

A · BOOK · OF

by Hosie and Leonard Baskin

DRAGONS

Alfred A. Knopf · New York

j398.6
B28b
C.1

This is a Borzoi Book published by Alfred A. Knopf, Inc.

Copyright © 1985 by Leonard Baskin.
All rights reserved under International and Pan-American Copyright Conventions.
Published in the United States by Pantheon Books, a division of Random House, Inc.,
New York, and simultaneously in Canada by Random House of Canada Limited, Toronto.
Manufactured in the United States of America • First Edition
2   4   6   8   10   9   7   5   3   1

Library of Congress Cataloging in Publication Data
Baskin, Hosie, A book of dragons.
Summary: Features twenty-two dragons from many mythologies and literatures,
including St. George's dragon, the Hydra, and Smaug from "Hobbit."
1. Dragons—Pictorial works—Juvenile literature.
[1. Dragons] I. Baskin, Leonard. II. Title.
GR830.D7B37   1985   398.2′454   85-6581
ISBN 0-394-86298-8   ISBN 0-394-96298-2 (lib. bdg.)

KN

MAY   '86

FOR LUKIE

from her loving brother and father

LEVIATHAN

Leviathan, a serpent-dragon so colossal that its coils encircle the earth, keeps its tail firmly trapped in its mouth, thus preventing the world from falling apart. Its coils are multicolored, with scales so bright that they outshine the sun. It feeds on other normal-sized dragons. Leviathan and its frightful nemesis Behemoth were created together, just at the moment the universe was being formed. It is said that on the Day of Judgment they will fight and kill each other. And the righteous of the world shall feed upon the flesh of Leviathan.

TIAMAT

In Babylonian legends of the earth's beginning, there was no land, gods, or people. There was only Apsu and Tiamat. Apsu was the spirit of fresh water and order and he was beautifully formed. Tiamat was the spirit of salt water and chaos and she had a splotchy bovine body, with the wings of an eagle and the head of an ox. Apsu and Tiamat had many offspring, and these became the first gods. But Apsu grew displeased with the children because they disturbed the peaceful quiet that ruled the universe. So he decided to destroy them. Tiamat pleaded with Apsu to spare their children's lives, but Apsu was adamant and refused. After learning of his father's intent, one of the young gods captured Apsu and killed him. Tiamat was furious, and determined to avenge her husband's murder. So she spawned a brood of fearsome creatures—giant serpents, roaring dragons, lion-demons and scorpion-men—and with them met Marduk, one of her godchildren, in combat. Marduk, armed with a fishing net and bolts of lightning, arrived to do battle in a chariot drawn by the four winds. He and Tiamat began by shouting insults and threats. Then, they fought. In a titanic struggle Marduk trapped Tiamat in his net and slew her with a fork of lightning.

DANIEL AND THE DRAGON

After the destruction of the temple at Jerusalem, Daniel and the Jews lived in exile in Babylon. Though the people of that land worshipped a mighty dragon, Daniel refused to. King Cyrus said to him, "This is no idol, for see, it eats and drinks and lives. You cannot claim that this is not a living god, so worship it." Daniel replied, "I will worship the Lord, my God, for he is the living, eternal God." He then offered to slay the dragon without using a sword or lance or weapon of any kind. The king consented to the contest. Daniel formed a ball out of pitch and fat and sulfur and fed this to the greedy, all-consuming dragon. The monster gulped it down and burst open, pieces of its burning flesh flying everywhere. Confronted by the dragon-god's catastrophic collapse and death, King Cyrus began to worship Daniel's God.

THE SHEN LUNG

The Shen Lung is the mightiest in power of the eight orders of Chinese Dragonhood. The realm of the Shen Lungs is the sky and the sea, all of earth's soil, the sun, and the moon. Good and bad weather are under their control. They hold the fortunes of all who work on land and sea. As the Shen Lung is incredibly powerful, so it is remarkably lazy. To avoid any sort of work, a Shen Lung can shrink to the size of a mouse and hide in out-of-the-way places in houses and trees. The Thunder god sends his servants to search for the lazy Shen Lungs. When they find one they punish it with bolts of lightning. That is why lightning often strikes trees and houses. Shen Lung is the Chinese New Year Good Luck Dragon that appears in parades and festivals. Wonderfully and variably colored, the Shen Lung has long streamers of hair, filaments of blue and red, green and gold, orange and yellow. Shimmering and shining, the Shen Lung vibrates and quivers in a trembling rainbow of brilliant colors as it moves along.

BEOWULF AND GRENDEL'S MOTHER

In the Dark Ages after the hero Beowulf mortally wounded the dragon Grendel, whose nightly murderous visits had terrorized Denmark, happiness returned to the land. But then Grendel's mother, a hideous cross between dragon and human, emerged from the dark lake where she lived to avenge her son's death. She went to the castle and carried off a Danish nobleman. Following the trail of blood, Beowulf set off in pursuit. On reaching the lake he swam down to the beast's lair. Taking the monster by surprise, he struck her with his sword. When the blow did nothing, he discarded his weapon and wrestled with her. But she proved too strong. She drew a knife and was about to kill Beowulf when he spied in the midst of her treasure hoard a magical sword that had been made in a giant's forge. Seizing this, Beowulf struck off her head with a mighty blow. Then seeing Grendel's body nearby, he severed its head; taking the great sword and head as trophies, he returned to the castle and became the hero of the land.

SMAUG

Smaug was a remarkably old dragon who lived in a gigantic cavern in the middle of the Lonely Mountains. He would lie for days in his cave, sprawling over his great piles of treasure, seemingly asleep, but with one eye barely open, watching for intruders. He was not always so quiet, however. When angered, he would fly out of his lair and destroy anything that crossed his path. After many years the area around the Lonely Mountains became so devoid of life that it became known as the Desolation of Smaug. Smaug's end came when he decided to revenge himself on a town that he believed had sent a three-foot-tall thief called Bilbo Baggins to raid his treasure hoard. As Smaug flew over the town terrorizing the inhabitants, a mighty archer called Bard sank a shaft deep into the only vulnerable part of his underbelly. And he plummeted to the ground dead.

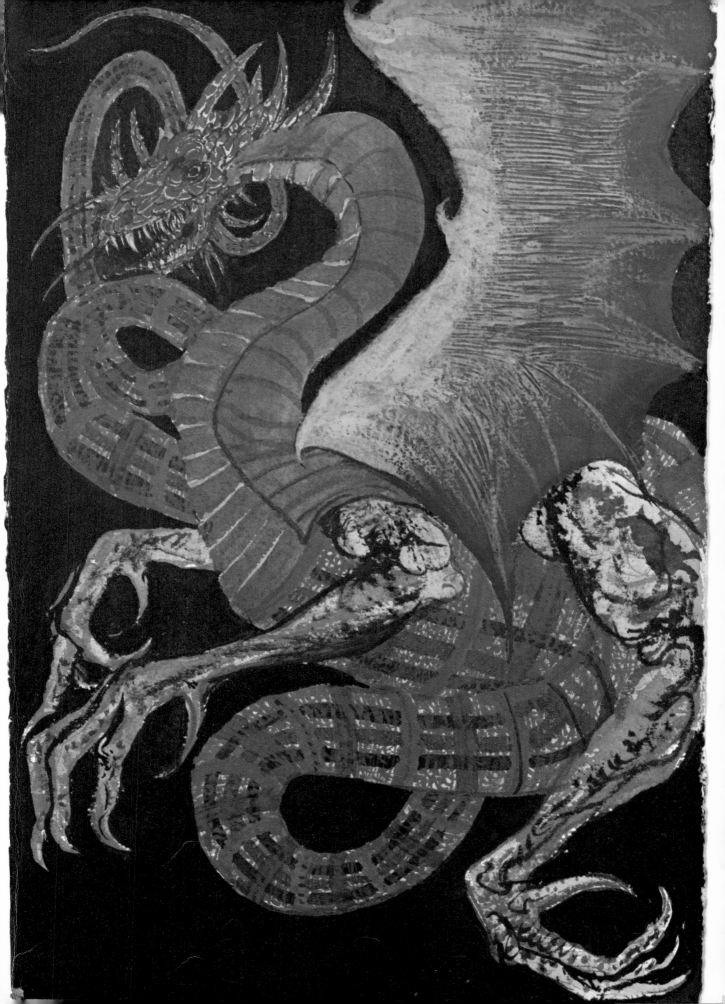

THE BASILISK

It is said that sometimes a very old rooster, well after it has lost all interest in hens, somehow miraculously manages to lay an egg; when that remarkable egg is hatched by a serpent or a toad, the terrible Basilisk is born. Its name means "prince," for it walks about on two feet with a stately motion, and its cockscomb looks likes a coronet or crown. Its natural voice is a hiss, which terrifies serpents, dragons, and all other creatures that hear it. The Basilisk has a terrible poison against which there is no cure, and its very look will kill. Like the Gorgon, the Basilisk is virtually indestructible. It can only be destroyed by forcing it to look at itself, by holding a mirror against it, thus turning it into stone. In size the Basilisk is not terribly imposing, but its fearsome powers more than make up for its diminutive frame.

THE LAIDLY WORM

In medieval England the realm of Northumbria was ruled by a king who had two children, Childe Wynd and Margaret. When Childe Wynd was grown, he left home to seek his fortune. Shortly thereafter the queen died, and the king remarried an evil woman who possessed magical powers. Jealous of her young stepdaughter's beauty, she put a curse on Margaret, turning her into an ugly writhing serpent, the Laidly Worm. And the queen croaked that the curse would last

"Until Childe Wynd, the king's own son,
Come to the Heugh and thrice kiss thee."

Banished from the castle, the Laidly Worm made its way to the Heugh of Spindleton, a nearby crag. And there she lived, wreaking havoc in the countryside and devouring everything she came across. When Childe Wynd learned that his kingdom was being terrorized by a dragon, he set out to destroy the beast. Following the dragon's tracks, he came to the Heugh and was just about to cut off its ugly head when the monster spoke:

"Quit your sword, unbend your bow,
And give me kisses three…
For though I am a poisonous worm,
No harm I'd do to thee."

Recognizing the voice as his beloved sister Margaret's, the prince threw down his sword and kissed the repulsive creature three times. The curse was broken, and the Laidly Worm vanished. In its place stood Margaret, and peace was restored to the kingdom.

THE FOLD-UP DRAGON

The Fold-up Dragon is a terrible coward. Unlike other dragons, it doesn't howl and growl. Nor does it take pleasure in terrifying other creatures or human beings; it actually avoids meeting all other living things, great or small. By folding its umbrella-like self tightly, it tucks itself into any handy crevice or hollowed-out tree. Or it simply finds a lonely, shaded place to quietly sit, trying to become invisible, disturbing no one, condemning nothing. The Fold-up Dragon survives on the pickings left by scary and hostile dragons. As it expends very little energy, because it mostly hides and sleeps, it can live a very long time on a very small amount of food. Since it is so bashful and retiring a dragon, there are virtually no legends about it.

FAFNIR

Fafnir began life as a giant. In his youth he killed his father to gain his treasure and then, through magical means, had himself transformed into a dragon, the better to guard the ill-gotten hoard. As Fafnir grew older, he became more and more vicious, terrorizing vast areas of Scandinavia, until finally the hero Siegfried dug a pit along the path that Fafnir used daily when he went to drink. Siegfried climbed down into the pit and waited with ready sword. In time the mighty dragon approached. When it passed directly over the pit, Siegfried plunged his weapon deep into the dragon's body. The dragon reared and lashed furiously with its tail as Siegfried leaped out of the pit and drove in the lethal blow. Fafnir collapsed onto the ground, twitched for a moment or two before dying, and the country was saved.

PERSEUS AND THE SEA DRAGON

Perseus, using the winged sandals that the god Hermes had lent him, was flying home to Greece after slaying Medusa when he passed over Ethiopia. There he saw a beautiful young black woman chained to a rock at the edge of the sea. She was the princess Andromeda, the daughter of King Cepheus, and she was being offered as a sacrifice to liberate her people from the devastations of a terrible sea dragon. When Perseus saw the dragon crouched, ready to devour the innocent princess, he flew down onto the monster's back and slew it with a single blow. That was the end of the sea dragon, but Perseus and Andromeda were married, and Andromeda bore him many beautiful children in whom the glory of Perseus lived on.

KRAK'S DRAGON

Around the year 700, the legendary Polish hero Krak was at the peak of his fame. His wanderings took him to the town of Wavel, where he found the inhabitants terrorized by a huge, malignant, birdlike dragon with immense purple wings. This dragon greedily demanded tributes of food and drink, leaving the townspeople to starve. Learning of their distress, Krak filled a sheepskin with saltpeter, sewed it up, and left it where the dragon would see it. The dragon found it and swallowed it whole. Ravaged by thirst, it drank half of the nearby river Vistula and burst into tiny pieces. Krak stayed to found the city of Krakow on the heights overlooking Wavel.

TARASQUE

In the middle years of the Dark Ages, near the town of Tarascon on the banks of the Rhône, there lived the Tarasque, a lumbering apelike creature with a fearsome feline head. It had terrible fangs, four bear paws, a hard, dense, spiky, colorful pelt, and the tail of a viper. One day the ugly beast, on one of its rare forays out of its cave, was in the midst of devouring a hapless peasant when Saint Martha appeared. Acting simply and fearlessly and with the deepest faith, Saint Martha took a vial and sprinkled holy water on the Tarasque. Magically it ceased devouring the peasant, stopped its roaring, and quelled its flames. It became tame and obedient. But the local people, lacking the saint's faith, set upon the now harmless Tarasque and killed it.

THE DRAGON OF COLCHIS

Jason, the rightful king of Thessaly in Greece, was sent by his usurping uncle and guardian, Pelias, to retrieve the Golden Fleece from far-off Colchis. He set sail in his ship, the *Argo,* with a crew of heroes, and after many perilous adventures they reached the land of Colchis. There King Aeetes gave Jason several tasks to perform in order to win the Golden Fleece. With the help of the king's daughter, the magician Medea, Jason successfully completed these tasks; then he confronted the problem of the fleece, which hung from a tree. Around the base of the tree was coiled a dragon which never slept. From poppy seeds, Medea made a magical potion which Jason sprinkled into the dragon's eyes, dripping it from a freshly cut juniper branch. When the beast fell asleep, Jason took the fleece. He and Medea returned to Thessaly with their prize and became king and queen, but they did not live happily ever after.

THE GHOSTLY DRAGON

Sightings of the Ghostly Dragon are very rare, but it is seen from time to time sitting against a late evening sky, appearing and disappearing before one's very eyes.

SAINT GEORGE

According to legend, Saint George was born in Coventry in the Middle Ages, the son of a certain Lord Albert. His mother died in childbirth, and soon thereafter the infant was kidnapped by a female enchanter called Kalyb, who reared him. When he came of age she gave him an impregnable suit of armor, and the young knight set off to seek his fortune. In time his travels took him to a place inhabited by a loathsome dragon, a monster that had repelled all the armies that had been set against it. As the dragon consumed more and more of the region, the people were forced to sacrifice their children to it; no child was spared, not even the king's only daughter, Sabra. When her time came, she dressed in her finest gown and walked with great courage away from the city toward the lake to the dreaded spot where she was to meet her end. Hearing of the princess' plight, Saint George had come to slay the dragon. Upon seeing the knight, the princess called, "Quickly mount your horse and fly, lest you perish with me." No sooner had she spoken these words than the loathsome dragon lifted its head above the waters of the lake. Sabra, trembling, cried, "Fly! Fly! Sir Knight." Instead, Saint George advanced upon the roaring, fire-breathing dragon and slew it. And Saint George and Sabra were married and lived in peace and happiness.

THE EIGHT-TAILED DRAGON

On one of his many travels, the mighty hero Susano journeyed through the Izumo province of Japan. When he was passing near the mouth of the river Hi, he observed an old couple sitting outside their cottage in tears. When Susano asked them why they were crying, they told him that their daughter, Kushinada-hime, was about to be sacrificed to a dragon which had eight tails, eight heads, and glowing red eyes, and was so immense that it filled an entire valley. It had come at this time every year for seven years and had already devoured Kushinada's seven older sisters. Now it was going to eat their last daughter. Susano offered to rescue Kushinada if she would consent to marry him. She agreed and he set up eight barrels of sake as bait. When the dragon arrived and saw the barrels, each head immediately drank one and fell into a deep, drunken sleep. Then Susano drew his sword and cut the dragon into little pieces. He and Kushinada were married and they lived together in happiness.

THE MANUSCRIPT DRAGON

This gorgeous and bejeweled dragon lives only in the magnificently illuminated pages of medieval manuscripts and books. It scampers across the opening of the Apocalypse of Saint John, frightening the woman clothed in the sun with a crown of twelve stars. It dutifully succumbs to Saint George, Saint Michael, and Saint Margaret. It happily allows Saint Simeon Stylites to remove an enormous stake from its eye. It becomes a vast winged serpent, slithering through blazing deserts or allowing Saint Marcel to lead it miles away from Paris and promising never to return. The Manuscript Dragon and one of its mates, posing as griffins, carry Alexander the Great through the air in his castle-shaped basket. It permits the Chevalier de Gozano, Grand Master of the Order of Saint John of Jerusalem, to extract the supposedly precious stone from its head.

Only in the pages of these illuminated books can you see travelers from Ethiopia luring dragons out of their caves, saddling them, and flying them back to Ethiopia to be butchered and eaten. Or Saint Margaret kill a dragon by making the sign of the cross. And where but in the habitat of the Manuscript Dragon can you see Saint Donatus spitting (in an unsaintly way) into a dragon's mouth, thus killing it and cleansing the water of a spring? The Manuscript Dragon stars in thousands of stories, but it has never been known to leave those beautiful books, until now.

LEONARD BASKIN

holds a special place in the book and art worlds. He was awarded the Caldecott Honor for *Hosie's Alphabet,* and *The New York Times* recognized *Leonard Baskin's Miniature Natural History* as a Best Illustrated Children's Book of the Year. He has been a recipient of the American Institute of Graphic Arts Gold Medal for his distinguished contribution to the graphic arts. And his sculptures and prints appear in many collections, including those of the National Gallery in Washington, D.C., the Museum of Modern Art and the Whitney Museum of American Art in New York, the Museum of Fine Arts in Boston, and the Vatican Museum in Rome. He is a visiting professor of art at Hampshire College and lives with his family in Leeds, Massachusetts.

HOSIE BASKIN

has been contributing to the texts of his father's books since *Hosie's Alphabet.* He has just completed his secondary education in England and has not had time to slay many dragons, but his interest in them inspired this book.